HOW I MAGICALLY
UNSTUCK MY LIFE
IN THIRTY CRAZY DAYS

HOW I MAGICALLY UNSTUCK MY LIFE IN THIRTY CRAZY DAYS

WITH BOB PROCTOR

BOOK 1

SANDY GALLAGHER

MEDIA

Published 2023 by Gildan Media LLC
aka G&D Media
www.GandDmedia.com

Front cover design by Patti Knoles

Interior design by Meghan Day Healey of Story Horse, LLC.

Library of Congress Cataloging-in-Publication Data is avail-
able upon request

ISBN: 978-1-7225-0600-1

10 9 8 7 6 5 4 3 2 1

For Bob Proctor

You taught me to spread love everywhere I go
by spreading love everywhere you went.
You are the magic in this story of hope.

Sandy

CHAPTER ONE
STUCK

Chloe hated the sound of her alarm clock. It had the grating quality of nails on a chalkboard, worming itself into her best dreams and soundest slumbers. What she hated most was once she slapped the off button and swung her legs out of bed, her day had nowhere to go but down.

When Chloe had moved from Arizona to California at the tender age of twenty-two, her dream had been to become an award-winning journalist, bringing awareness of important issues to the people, making a difference in the world. A big difference.

Los Angeles had other ideas, among them the cost of living. Every studio apartment in a decent neighborhood was out of her price range. She considered roommates, but hated the idea of living with another human. She settled for a studio in Pacoima the size of a closet, a stone's throw from the freeway. The thunder of vehicles and their incessant honking were right outside her window, a constant reminder of her plight.

It's only temporary, she told herself, squeezing her possessions into the tiny, one-room living space. As soon as she had a job at a big-time news outlet, she would move into a much nicer place. Hopefully, a neighborhood without bars on the windows. She could dream.

Chloe had spent weeks applying for every journalist job she could find, to no avail. As her savings dwindled to nothing, she decided to listen to her mother and find a job at a local station back home. At the last moment, she got an offer to become a sports columnist. The pay was less than she'd hoped for, and meant she would have to stay in her small apartment for a little longer. At least the job paid the bills and allowed her to stay in her dream city.

That had been six years ago. Chloe had risen in the company somewhat, moving from the sports column to assistant editor, giving her more responsibility and a slight wage increase. She had moved from her studio apartment into a one-bedroom in the same complex, still far from where she'd dreamed she would be. With the added responsibility came more work hours, killing her social life. With no prospects for upward mobility, and no time for anything but the daily grind, she was stuck.

You're not stuck. This is just life, Chloe sighed. *How are you not used to it by now?* That small, ugly voice had taken up permanent residence in her head, a lifetime culmination of struggle, self-doubt, and poor self-image. The older she grew, the more she was forgetting that she'd ever lived without it.

Even if I did have some free time, I don't have anywhere to go, she thought, continuing her daily internal refrain. Straining into a pair of slacks she'd found on sale, she frowned at the swell of tummy that hung over the waistline. Nearing thirty, she no longer had any interest in the party scene, and eating out at a restaurant meant paying for a meal with money she didn't have.

She had a few friends in the area, but they all had jobs that didn't allow for much free time either. Her dating life wasn't much better. Her last boyfriend had pledged his undying love. He wasn't particularly special or intelligent, but he had been kind and funny and seemed like a possible fit, until she found his social media page and pictures of his wife. She considered trying one of those dating apps her friend Ashley had used to find her boyfriend, but the thought of wading through countless incompatible profiles didn't appeal to her in the least. Stuck, stuck, stuck.

Chloe brushed her dark brown hair back and pulled it back in a sensible ponytail. When she'd moved to L.A., full of hope and optimism, she'd worn her hair down. That was long ago, the efforts of an idealistic kid she no longer recognized. Slipping her comfortable work shoes on, her stomach growled. How was she going to lose that ten pounds? How much longer until she admitted it was more like fifteen? She grabbed a protein bar and stuffed it into her purse, locking the door and the iron security door on her way out.

Chloe's beat-up Pontiac grumbled and sputtered awake as she turned the key in the ignition. Glancing at the fuel gauge, she sighed. She'd have to stop on the way to work. She hoped she had room left on one of her credit cards.

The elevator let out the same off-key *ding* as it opened onto the drab office space, gray carpet and beige cubicles of L.A. Local News, as soulless as their faded white walls. The small digital news outlet covered major stories affecting Los Angeles County, along with the usual celebrity gossip. It made the bulk of its money covering the local scene, community events and school sports, mostly.

After years of wearing her boss down, she convinced him to try a weekly editorial series, the *Friday Edition*. It had gained some traction, becoming an audience favorite and one of the only aspects of her job she actually enjoyed.

The din of a busy newsroom permeated the stale air as people hurried to wrap up another week. The office kept a skeleton crew on the weekends except for major breaking news and local sports, so bulking up the website with content to last through Monday was always a rush. Patty, the office manager, peeked her head up over a cubicle wall and waved her over.

Holding up a finger, Chloe moved to her own five-by-five slice of heaven, setting her purse and messenger bag on her desk. Flicking on her screen, she plopped down in her cheap office chair and took a breath. Everyone she knew hated Mondays, but Fridays were the worst for her. She was always exhausted from the night before, staying up too late to bang out the final draft of her latest *Friday Edition* piece. Her boss, Frank, was a stickler with the editing, and they always ended up arguing about the tone and message she was trying to convey.

Sticking a flash drive in a port, she opened the piece and double-checked the last few paragraphs. Happy with it, she emailed it to Frank. He didn't seem to have a problem with her first drafts. He just enjoyed the confrontation. Perhaps he needed it. He thrived on the energy of countless challenges. She hoped today he would approve the draft without making any last-minute adjustments before he handed it over to Ed, the website manager, for publishing. Never knowing how her work came out until reading it online was always irritating.

She understood his process. As assistant editor, she often did the same with everyone else's stories. With Frank, it felt personal. He'd likely say it was just professional development or something. She wished he would turn it off for the *Friday Edition*. She actually cared about those stories.

Pulling herself slowly out of her chair, Chloe grabbed her bag and made her way down the aisle to Patty's cube. On the way, she pondered how everyone at L.A. Local was either too young to feel as she did, or too old to remember they ever had. A pang of anxiety shot up from her midsection at the thought of becoming the latter. The place had a way of making its occupants as dreary and washed-out as itself, nothing more than nondescript fixtures in their own lives.

Patty was firmly fixed in the latter category. "G'morning, sunshine," the aged woman said.

"Hey Patty, what's up?" Chloe replied, already knowing the answer.

Peering over her half-glasses, Patty flicked her chin up and to the left, indicating Frank's office in the back corner. "The usual. His lordship has summoned you."

"Lucky me."

Frank's corner office was its own kind of cubicle, though it had windows and a little more breathing room. It was every bit the trap the rest of the place was. If Chloe wasn't careful, she'd occupy it herself someday.

"Hey, Frank."

"Hey," he said, frowning at his computer screen half-buried by the detritus of an overflowing desk. "Close the door. I can't hear myself think."

A hefty man of fifty, with a circle of dark hair left on his scalp and a salt-and-pepper goatee, Frank reminded Chloe of a monk. A miserable one. Small, round glasses rested above a bulbous nose, and his white button-up strained against his generous belly, the dingy shirt looking both smooth and wrinkled at the same time.

He took a sip from a mug as old as L.A. itself, scowling. "Ugh, we need a new coffee maker. Doesn't help that this is yesterday's coffee."

"There's the shop around the corner. I could send someone." Closing the door and taking a seat, Chloe felt like there was no need to say anything. She knew what he was going to say.

"Sure," Frank snorted, "and while you're at it, have them grab some steak and lobster for lunch. Enough small talk. I've got a story for you. A strange one."

"Sounds good." Chloe dug her notebook and pen from her bag. Most of her coworkers used digital recorders, but she still preferred the old-fashioned method. "Strange is good. What is it, another school event or something?"

Hoping beyond hope, she thought of last year, when she'd written an article about a local high school football team who had put the school district's first female quarterback on the field.

The story had done well and website traffic saw a significant increase. Female subscriptions bumped fifteen percent. A few of her early pieces had done equally well, all leading to her promotion, but that football story had really stuck with her. She cared about the story, what it meant and the people in it. She was always on the hunt for more stories like it. They were a true rarity in the wasteland of sports scores, traffic reports, and meaningless red-carpet events that made up the majority of her content.

"Not this time," Frank said, swiping at an unidentifiable stain on his shirt. "There's this big shot woman, Sarah Garner. She's speaking at the Hilton today. Some sort of talk about people flocking to her for secrets to a successful life. Ever hear of her?"

Chloe grimaced. "Nope. Is she legit?"

"I don't know, I'm not sure what legit is in this space. All I know is she's packing them in. She's whipping around the country on her private jet, holding events for some institute she founded. She's got a massive online following and a slew of high-profile clients singing her praises. She's a pretty big deal. If it's malarky, she's better than most."

"Hm. I guess I'm just surprised you want to cover this sort of thing."

"That's the strange part," Frank said, eyeing her. "They specifically requested you."

Chloe's eyebrows shot up. "What?"

"That's what I said. It's a private event. The tickets are sold via her website. We're the only press they've invited. This Garner chick is on a multi-city tour, promoting some idea of hers. And get this. Tickets for every stop sold out in hours. There's a waiting list a mile long to see this woman."

"Why invite press at all? They don't need promotion. Least of all from some local news website. It sounds like they could get the L.A. Times if they wanted. Why bother with us?"

"I'd take offense if you weren't so right. Hell, we don't get invited anywhere. Remember the new dealership that opened last year?"

"Yeah, you told me to just show up and see what happened. They didn't kick me out, so we ran the story. But, why me?"

Frank shrugged. "I have no idea, but hey, you may get an exclusive interview out of this which would be nice. Might be an interesting story, probably not. Your job is to show up. Apparently, this thing goes on all weekend, but that's not gonna happen for you. If you do get an interview with Garner, tell them it needs to be today. There's nothing about her you can't learn in an afternoon, and I'm not paying overtime for a story our audience might not care about. Plus, I need you at Chatsworth High tomorrow for the Saturday game."

"What if this turns out to be all talk and no substance? And what about the editing for the weekend content?"

"I'll take care of the editing. As for Garner, I'm leaving it up to you. Get a lay of the land and make the call. If it's worth sticking around, go for it. If not, wrap it up and head back. There's plenty of other stuff going on." He shrugged. "Worst case scenario, you spend a Friday out of the office. Best case scenario, you work your magic and get us another bump in the numbers."

"You got it," Chloe said, stowing her notebook in her bag and heading for the door.

"Oh, by the way." Frank hesitated, wincing. "Keep track of any expenses. I'll reimburse you. Maybe."

CHAPTER TWO

THE HILTON

Los Angeles traffic was as hectic as ever, but Chloe was able to make her way to the Hilton on South Grand Avenue without too much trouble. Since Frank was footing the bill for expenses, she decided to valet rather than trying to find a parking space and walking two blocks.

"Welcome to the Hilton." A valet attendant trotted up in a powder-blue collared shirt and khaki slacks before Chloe had finished opening her door. He was older than the rest of the attendants. His Hilton name tag read *Kim*. "Are you going to need help with your luggage, Miss?"

"Oh, I don't have any luggage. L.A. Local News." Chloe pulled out her press badge. "I'm supposed to be covering the Sarah Garner event."

"Of course, Miss." Kim took her keys with a nod. "That'll be in the main conference room. Just walk in through the double doors and follow the signs. You can't miss it. Name, please?"

"Chloe Daniels."

Kim scribbled her name on a ticket, tore off the stub, and handed it to her. "When you're ready, just bring your ticket to the cashier desk over there." He pointed to a podium where a bored-looking girl stood at a computer texting. "We'll have it brought up right away."

"Thanks much," Chloe said, heading toward the huge double-glass doors of the entrance. A blast of cool air hit her as she stepped into the lobby. White walls, marble floors, and high ceilings greeted her. Hundreds of people milled around, most wearing lanyards for the Sarah Garner event.

Looks like I'm in the right place, Chloe thought. She followed the signs to the conference room, where a security guard in a Hilton uniform stopped her. She flashed her press badge and gave him her name.

He checked his clipboard, nodding. "Ah, Miss Daniels. Thank you for coming. I've been instructed to alert Miss Garner's assistant of your arrival." He put a hand to his earpiece. "Joyce, the reporter has arrived. Yes, ma'am." He opened the door to the conference room, gesturing her through. "Joyce will meet you inside momentarily."

"Thank you," Chloe replied.

The large, rectangular conference room was lined with hundreds of cushioned folding chairs, bifurcated by a narrow center aisle. A wide stage sat at the far end, raised a few feet above the luxurious carpet. A blank projection screen hung from the wall overlooking the stage. Several long tables lined the perimeter of the room, offering refreshments and reading materials. Bustling with activity, small groups of people mingled as others chose their seats. Chloe's skin tingled a bit with the buzz.

As she decided where to sit, a tall woman in a sharp designer pantsuit approached her, hand outstretched. "Hi, you must be Chloe. I'm Joyce, Sarah's assistant. Thanks so much for coming."

Chloe smiled, shaking her hand. "It's my pleasure. I understand you asked for me."

Joyce nodded, flicking a strand of bright-red hair away from her eye. "Yes, we did. One of our interns came across that article you wrote about the high school football team. We were quite moved by it, and Sarah asked us to track you down to see if you'd be interested in writing a little story on our event here this weekend."

"Oh, wow," Chloe said. "That's . . . surprising."

"Only the first surprise of many, we hope," Joyce replied. She laughed at Chloe's puzzled expression. "We'll be having a break around lunchtime, and Sarah would like to speak with you then, if you're agreeable. She'll be able to tell you more. If you decide you want to write something on your time with us for L.A. Local, Sarah will be happy to answer some questions. How's that sound?"

"That sounds perfect, thank you."

"Excellent," Joyce said, checking her watch. "We'll be starting shortly, so you'll have to excuse me." She pointed to a door near the stage, under the watchful eye of another security guard. "Just speak to security at intermission, and she'll bring you through to us."

"Wonderful, I'll do that."

They shook hands again. "It's a real pleasure to meet you, Chloe. Look forward to chatting soon. In the meantime, enjoy the event, and feel free to interview any willing participants."

"Great, thanks again," Chloe replied. "Pleasure meeting you, too."

Eyeing the many rows of seats, Chloe decided on one about four rows back, affording her a good view of the stage. A three-ring binder had been placed on each chair. She grabbed it before sitting, wondering what kind of information was inside.

A few seats over, a stout, blonde woman in a colorful dress and embroidered shawl buzzed with excitement. "Are you as excited as I am?" the woman asked as Chloe took out her notebook and pen.

"It's my first event, actually," Chloe replied.

"Oh, well, you're in for a treat," the woman gushed. "My name's Kendra. I first attended her Unstuck in Thirty Days event a few months ago. When I heard she was in town again on tour, I just had to come. I think it'll be a really good refresher for me, and I wanted to hear the lessons again from my new perspective, to see if I could learn anything more." She smiled. "Takes a little work to get unstuck, you know."

Chloe raised an eyebrow. "Thirty days? How does she cover it all in a single weekend?"

"Well," Kendra explained, "When you leave, there are six lessons, each taking five days to fully explore and absorb. Everyone here is at different stages of the experience. Today's talk covers lessons one and two, tomorrow's covers three and four, then five and six on Sunday. With that kind of overlap, it helps everyone, no matter where they're stuck. She reaffirms what they've already learned, exploring where they're at now, and gives them a preview of what's to come. She is such a force of nature. I'm telling you. If you ever were looking for a moment that might change your life, you've found it."

"Sounds exciting," Chloe said, trying to match the woman's upbeat tone.

"It is," Kendra continued. "I've watched all the online lectures and livestreams as well, but there's just something about seeing her in real life. So inspiring!"

"I'm writing an article for L.A. Local News," Chloe explained. "Do you mind if I jot some of this down?"

"Oh, how cool, absolutely! Quote anything you want! I've never been in the paper before." Kendra took her phone out of her purse and held it up. "Selfie with me?"

Chloe smiled. "Sure. And the article will be on our website. Question for you. Would you say this woman has helped you?"

"More than help me," Kendra said, nodding. "Lots of people help me. This woman has mattered to me. Before I attended Sarah's lectures, I was barely making a living working two part-time jobs. She gave me the confidence to start my own arts and crafts business. Now my hobby is my full-time job, and I am absolutely loving it!" She held out her shawl for Chloe to see. "Do you like it? I made it myself."

Chloe inspected the shawl, covered in intricate hand-stitched patterns of birds and flowers. She had to admit, it was beautiful. "Wow, that's lovely, Kendra. Look at this. Such detail."

"Thank you so much," Kendra said, blushing. She dropped her voice, almost embarrassed, and whispered, "I sell pieces like this for four figures."

Chloe's eyebrows shot up. "That's amazing."

"I know!" Kendra said, laughing. "I know! I even have a waiting list. I'm in the process of expanding. First time in my life I have had employees. I never imagined something I loved so much I could turn into a business, let alone a successful one. It's because of Sarah. It's so much more than just earning money. She changes the way you think about yourself, and how you matter. She has this unusual gift to affect your life." She settled her shawl back over her shoulders. "Expect the impossible."

"That's wonderful to hear," Chloe said, smiling. "I hope so, too." *But I doubt it,* her small, tired voice chimed in.

The lights dimmed, and Kendra wriggled in her seat. "It's starting!" she whispered. The audience rose to their feet, applauding as a woman in a dark-blue pantsuit and black heels strode onto the stage. The welcoming music and thunderous welcome was deafening.

"Hello and welcome," Sarah Garner smiled with her arms out, welcoming her crowd with genuine enthusiasm. Her voice was softly spirited, amplified by a lapel microphone. Her features were smooth and elegant, her lustrous brown hair falling to her shoulders, framing dark eyes and a bright smile highlighted by soft touches of natural makeup. She was magnetic.

"It is so wonderful to see all of you here today. I celebrate your decision to unstuck your life starting today." She held her hand across her forehead shielding her eyes from the glare of the spotlights and looked out over the audience. "I see some of you have a copy of my book *How I Magically*

Unstuck My Life in Thirty Crazy Days. Thank you very much for that. If you stay after on Sunday, I'll hold back and sign it."

A small cheer went up, and Sarah laughed. "Whether this is your second or third time with us, are currently in the middle of getting unstuck, or your first time, thank you all for coming. We have an exciting three days planned for you, featuring insights and conversations that haven't appeared on our website or in any of our live streaming events. We will have Q&A sessions at the end of each day, so save your best questions so we can all share. Our goal is to offer you a deeper understanding of how you can use these new ideas to become your best self.

"For those new to the program, let me say this. Sixteen years ago, this thinking was new to me, too. I was an experienced, successful lawyer, climbing the corporate ladder, when I happened to attend a lecture by Bob Proctor. I didn't know it at the time, but Bob would become one of my dearest friends and mentors. His lecture sparked something in me that was waiting to bust out. Even though I was successful, I wanted to live a different sort of life.

"After a few more conversations with Bob, I decided there was more I wanted out of this one life I have been given. I settled up with my law firm, and began to change the way I thought about everything. It was the most important moment of my life.

"So when I walk out here this morning, and see you all, I see me, sitting on the edge of a life I could never imagine." She took a step back on the stage and wiped a tear off her cheek. "I see me. I see you. And I know what this moment will mean for some of you."

The crowd erupted with applause and jumped to their feet. Chloe found it impossible not to join them. As she applauded, she was holding back tears and didn't know why. Sarah was touching something deep inside.

Sarah paused, growing solemn. "Bob passed away, recently. We had been friends for sixteen years. It's difficult on the days I want to pick up the phone and talk to him, remembering I no longer can.

"Over the years, when he and I learned of the passing of friends or colleagues, he would always remind me that death is not something to be sad about. We all come and go. It's part of our sacred journey. When someone passes from the physical world, they remain with us in spirit. I continue to remind myself of his words, especially on the days I miss him the most.

"I use these talks to celebrate his life. In this way, he is always with me, and now with you. "Let them see you," Bob would tell me. "Let them see what you have become." Sarah smiled and held her arms out wide. "So, here I am. Let's start celebrating."

The crowd applauded again, showing their appreciation for Sarah's friend and mentor.

"Let's get right into it. This first half day will focus on a brief overview of our time together and a glimpse into the first few of our six conversations. Before we dive in, I'd like to invite you all to close your eyes and take a deep breath. Let go, just for a few minutes. Let go of your worries, your questions, your concerns, even your goals. Let go of the gas bill, the cranky boss and the busted tailpipe. Set aside your daily life, your short-term and long-term plans, your fears and your wants. Now take another breath."

Playing along, Chloe peeked through an eye, looking around. The crowd was sitting motionless, eyes closed, some with their heads down. Sighing, she followed suit, trying to concentrate.

"Now," Sarah continued, "imagine that you're capable of doing things beyond your wildest imagination. Don't worry about the how, other than to know that you have infinite resources at your disposal. You are able to accomplish anything you desire. You are amazing. As I look out at you this moment, your power and potential is breathtaking.

"What comes to your mind? What is it you want to do? Where does your mind and your heart go when provided with limitless opportunity?" She paused, allowing the audience to ponder. "Okay, open your eyes." The audience stirred, bringing their attention back to Sarah as she wandered the stage. Her hands clasped behind her back, she studied several audience members, gauging the exercise's effect on them. "Where would your passion lead you if you could do anything in the world? This weekend, we're going to begin to make that answer a reality."

CHAPTER THREE

A Worthy Ideal

"Like many of the best things in life," Sarah continued, "what we are talking about this morning is easy to learn, challenging to master. Why? Because becoming your best self is never easy." She looked out over the audience, shook her head and smiled. "We know life can be difficult. With the right tools, living a life you love is within reach.

"We're going to be covering a short list of important topics over six easily digestible conversations. After this conference, if you devote just five days to each lesson, you'll find yourself in a completely new frame of mind after thirty days."

Sarah walked over to a table and held up a binder to the audience. "Take a look at the binder you've been provided. Not a lot of heft to it, is there? How can this handful of notes and worksheets require thirty days of my time? Surely, I can rip through this information in a single weekend.

"Of course you can, and we will. We're going to dive in with both feet, and you're going to learn a lot. The key to our time together comes later, after the weekend, when you've settled back into your daily routine. You'll go through it again, spending five days on each lesson. Reread each one. Think, dig into the nuance, the layers of meaning contained within.

"You'll rewrite the exercises, refining them as you glean more insights from the reading and each day discovering more about yourself. Review, rethink, rewrite. Every day for thirty days, and you'll feel your world transforming before your eyes." Sarah stopped and smiled. "One is never prepared for the power of the sacred imagination to awaken a life."

The auditorium was stone silent, hanging on every word filled with the sounds of people breathing. She was unwrapping the dreams of each and every one.

"You're going to hear me say that a lot this weekend. Review, rethink, rewrite. Review, rethink and rewrite."

She walked to the edge of the stage and smiled. "Oh my, I just forgot what I said. Could you remind me?

"Review, rethink and rewrite!" the crowd responded in unison. "Review, rethink, rewrite!" The crowd applauded again as Sarah held her arms straight and clapped, mouthing silently to the crowd, "wonderful!"

Chloe shifted in her seat. She was captivated by Sarah and the rapport she was building with the crowd. She knew she was meant to be here.

"What are our six takeaways?" She held up a finger for each as she listed them. "First, we'll be unlocking your imagination to talk about goals, what they are and how you keep choosing the wrong ones. We will talk about the difference between knowing and doing. We will discuss paradigms, maybe my favorite—what they are and how to evolve them. We will chat about the secrets of your conscious and subconscious mind.

Of course, we have to spend time on unleashing your own unique genius. I will show you how to tap into your higher mental faculties to shape your circumstances. Finally, we will end up talking about the power of your self-image and how to master it.

"Sounds simple enough, right?" The crowd laughed together.

"I will make you a promise."

Sarah walked to the edge of the stage and looked out at the faces of the crowd. "I make you a promise right here and now. This weekend, if you let me in, together we will unlock the life of your dreams."

The crowd leapt to its feet again with thunderous applause. Chloe was standing with them.

Sarah stepped back and quieted her audience with her arms. "I know. I want it, too. For each of you. Let's get the ball rolling by taking a look at the first two ideas. Our first conversation I call *a worthy ideal, how to set and achieve worthy goals.*"

Chloe set her notebook down and opened her binder as Sarah continued on. Less than an inch thick, it contained literature and worksheets for each of the six lessons, all laid out in an organized, easy-to-read fashion. A quote from Napoleon Hill stood at the top of lesson one. She recognized the name. He wrote *Think and Grow Rich*, a classic book on self-improvement. She'd never read it, having given up long ago on the thought of getting rich, or even improving herself. At this point, she'd settle for staying ahead of her bills.

"Those who reach decisions promptly and definitely, know what they want, and generally get it. The leaders in every walk of life decide quickly and firmly. That is a major reason why they are leaders. The world has a habit of making room for the person whose words and actions show they know where they are going."

Chloe couldn't argue with that. Leader or not, it sounded like good advice for everyone. She tuned back in to Sarah while jotting some notes.

"Let's begin with what I call your limiting beliefs," Sarah was saying. "Is it that you can't achieve the goal, or is it that you *believe* you can't achieve the goal? You'll see some questions in your binder on this. I encourage you to start on these written sections during our breaks and in the evenings. You'll also find blanks in the back, allowing you to write out more, which I can't recommend enough. As I've said, review, rethink, rewrite.

"We tend to make goals we know we can achieve. You can afford a new car this year, and you'd like to buy one? That's not a goal, that's a task. You already KNOW you can accomplish it.

"We call those Type A goals. Let's say you want a car this year, but you have your eye on one that's just out of your budget. You might be able to pull it off, and so you've set your sights on making it happen. That's a Type B goal, something you THINK you can do.

"What you and I are talking about is your Type C goals. These are the ginormous ones, what you really want, even if they seem way out of reach. Some of you call them fantasies. But you know what?" She smiled and wagged her finger at the crowd. "Some of them aren't fantasies at all. With the power of your imagination, many can be and will be yours.

"When you believe and are willing to do whatever it takes, you will move your ginormous goal from fantasy to theory. As you dedicate your mind and heart to this journey, believing with every fiber that it can be made reality, it will change your behavior."

She put her hand over her heart. "Believe me, I am living proof. With enough time, commitment, and improved behavior, your theory becomes fact. Fantasy, theory, fact. It all comes together through a fundamental change in what you believe, about yourself, the world around you, and the limitless potential flowing just below the surface of your current way of thinking. Think you are able to do it? Are you willing to do whatever it takes?"

"Yes, yes, yes," could be heard throughout the room. "Yes!"

Chloe continued jotting notes, wishing she'd brought a highlighter for the binder. She shook her head, realizing she was getting into it. *Imagine what Frank would say,* her disappointing voice chimed in, *you, buying into this stuff.*

Oh, stop it, she snapped back, surprising herself. *Frank isn't here. I am.*

After a few anecdotes and some more detail on lesson one, Chloe was surprised to hear Sarah say, "Well, it's almost noon now, so we're going to take an hour break for lunch. We'll be back at one. In the meantime, give some thought to the goal card in your binder. The first step to making your fantasy a reality is to write it down on your goal card, and always keep it with you. Make your Type C goal a part of your everyday life. Thanks so much, everyone! I'll see you at one o'clock."

There was more applause. Everyone stood and began collecting their belongings.

"What do you think? Pretty amazing, huh," Kendra asked as she retrieved a large handbag from under her seat. "I love how she challenges the views we've been raised to believe. It seems so obvious when she says it. I never noticed before, is all."

"It's certainly interesting," Chloe agreed. "I'm supposed to have a face-to-face interview with her right about now." She gathered up her bag. "Wish me luck."

Kendra gasped. "You lucky duck! Tell her I said hello. And good luck!"

"Thanks, I'll tell her. See you soon."

Chloe found the exit near the stage. After showing her badge to the security guard at the side entrance, the woman opened the door and led Chloe down a short hallway. The guard knocked on a random door, and Joyce answered.

The guard smiled. "Chloe Daniels for Sarah Garner."

"Wonderful, thank you so much," Joyce said. She opened the door wider, stepping aside for Chloe. "Please come in. Sarah is looking forward to meeting you."

Stepping into a small conference room lined with windows, Chloe found Sarah at a small sitting area in front of a flatscreen TV built into the far wall. The woman looked up from her phone and smiled, standing with an outstretched hand as Chloe made her way past the long conference table.

"Chloe, it's so nice to finally meet you," Sarah said.

"Likewise, Sarah," Chloe replied, shaking her hand. "Thank you for meeting with me."

"I'm going to go make sure we're set up for the second half," Joyce said. "Call if you need anything."

"Thank you, Joyce," Sarah said as the woman left. She gestured to the plush leather chair next to her own. "Please, sit. So, what do you think of the conference so far? Is it anything you and L.A. Local are interested in sharing?"

Chloe fished her pen and notepad out of her bag after sitting down. "It's definitely interesting. I do think it's worth sharing with our audience."

Sarah squinted at her, a playful look in her eye. "I'm thinking you don't usually go for this self-help stuff. Am I right?"

"You got me," Chloe replied with a laugh. "I mean, I'm open to it, I suppose. But after hearing you speak, I'm thinking my reservations have more to do with the circumstances than the content."

"How so?"

"Well," Chloe hesitated, gesturing vaguely. "Why me? Joyce said you liked one of my articles, but I don't see how that qualifies me to cover your event. Not when you could have any number of journalists throughout L.A."

Sarah nodded. "I thought that might be of concern, so allow me to explain. Like many businesses and organizations, the vast majority of my company's marketing is through word of mouth. We do a lot of online marketing and social media, of course, and we've appeared in a great many major publications over the years.

"We're at a point where the word of mouth does all the heavy lifting. That allows us to pick and choose where and when we invite the press, and most important of all, whom we invite.

"After reading your article on the local football team with the female player, we could tell you were someone worth inviting. Do you realize the impact that kind of writing can have on people?"

Chloe shrugged. "It did pretty well for us. Website traffic and subscriptions went up by a surprising margin, but those metrics tend to plateau and even fall away over time."

"Yes, but why did they go up in the first place? Because of how your story resonated with readers. You showed a great deal of empathy in your writing, Chloe. It's clear you poured your heart into that piece. It was a small story that you elevated in a meaningful way. You show why it mattered what happened on that football field in a small high school in a corner of America. Not something you see from many journalists these days. Least of all from someone so talented at her craft." She paused, giving Chloe a piercing look. "You are an exceptional writer."

Chloe fidgeted, feeling like the woman could see right through her, past all her defenses, into her very heart. She fumbled for something to say.

Sarah waved a hand. "I'm sorry, I tend to be more blunt than I should be. It puts people off."

"It's okay, I'm just . . . not used to hearing feedback like that."

"I see. Well, I think you should get used to it. But to answer your question, *that's* why I wanted to work with you. I'm not interested in getting the most exposure possible from the largest publications. The Institute and Unstuck are growing faster than we can keep up. We're focused on increasing the dialogue around the topic of personal and professional improvement. We want to reach people like you, who haven't really considered it, not to turn you into clients, but to get you thinking about it."

She poured some tea from a pot on the coffee table into two mugs. "There's a lack of hope these days, Chloe. My mission is to remind people that life can be better. I want to remind them that they ARE better. If you bring even a fraction of your talent to this story, you will help me make great strides toward that goal."

Chloe cleared her throat. "Well, you certainly know how to woo journalists."

Sarah laughed. "I'm merely sharing my observations. How is it a writer of your talent finds herself at a paper like L.A. Local?" She held up a hand. "Not that there's anything wrong with the outlet, if that's where you choose to be. But especially after perusing some of your other stories, I have to admit that it seems an odd fit."

Chloe shrugged again. "It's not my ideal job, but it pays the bills. When I get time, I send out the occasional resume, but the competition is crazy." She paused, what else to say. "Moving to L.A. six years ago, I definitely didn't think I'd wind up here. But here I am."

"Stuck?"

Chloe stared at the steam rising from her mug on the table and nodded her head. "Stuck."

"Remember the Type C goals we were talking about? The fantasies? What's your Type C goal?"

"Oh, I don't know," Chloe said, feeling the heat rise in her face. "I haven't filled out the goal card yet."

"It's okay, you don't have to tell me. I'm not here to pressure you into the experience, or try to convince you that it works. You will make that determination for yourself. Maybe at some point over the weekend, you'll feel comfortable enough to answer that question."

"That reminds me. My boss, Frank, is giving me today only for this story. I have to cover some local sports this weekend. I'm afraid I won't be able to attend the rest of the conference. But I am interested. I planned to see what you have online and probably sign up for some video courses."

"Hm," Sarah mused. "Let me ask you this. If you could attend the entire weekend, would you?"

"I would, yes."

"How about this? Tell Frank that if he allows you to attend the rest of the weekend, I'll give

L.A. Local an exclusive one-hour video interview. Provided you're the interviewer, of course."

"Wow, that's very generous of you. I still have to convince him that our audience would even be interested in the story. He's not very . . . open to this stuff."

Sarah smiled. "Not a problem. In addition to the interview, tell him my Institute would be willing to buy advertising in L.A. Local for, say, a year. I'll have Joyce write up an offer with the specifics. How's that sound?"

Chloe's eyebrows shot up. "That's, wow. Uh, okay." She paused, shaking her head. "But wait, why would you commit to a contract like that just to have me write this story? You don't know if it'll resonate with our audience any more than we do. It could turn out to be a complete waste of your time and money."

"Not at all. The evidence I need is right in front of me. Your audience responds to your writing. They'll respond to this. It's not the topic that matters, Chloe. It's the messenger."

Chloe nodded. "Hope."

"Hope." Sarah repeated.

"Okay. I'll talk to him."

"Wonderful!" Sarah said, standing. "Now, I have a number of calls to make, and I need to review the afternoon's material. Joyce will find you before the start of the afternoon session to see where we stand. However this goes, I'd like to see you again at the end of today's session, if you're willing."

"Absolutely," Chloe said, gathering her things as she stood.

They shook hands again. "Chloe, I like you very much. Thank you for being here and sharing your gift with me." Chloe nodded and tried not to cry. She was moved.

Sarah led her back to the conference room. Standing there, bewildered, watching as various groups mingled and laughed around their plates of finger food, Chloe couldn't help the broad smile that spread across her face. Advertising. Frank was going to love that.

CHAPTER FOUR
THE GOAL

"WHAT?!" Frank shouted.

Chloe held her phone away from her ear, glancing at the mingling crowd from a corner of the conference room. She noticed Joyce laughing with a small group, hoping she'd be able to bring the woman some good news. Frank was flipping his lid, all right, but not in the way she'd planned. "Frank, listen—"

"No, YOU listen! The football team playing tomorrow is the same one you wrote the article on. The girl's been made the starting quarterback. She's *starting*, Chloe! Do you realize what that means? It's the perfect time to capitalize on your first article. The bump in numbers will be double the first one."

"But the advertising."

"Oh, the advertising." Frank's voice dripped with sarcasm. "You think this is the first advertising offer I've had dangled in front of me? It's a garbage deal, believe me. They'll throw us a pittance in exchange for some ad space, and our numbers won't move a single digit. It's a red herring, Chloe. The Unstuck conference story is a shot in the dark, at best. The football story is a sure thing. You're going to that game."

"But couldn't Eddie write it and I'll edit it?"

"You know damn well follow-up articles don't do as well when they're written by another reporter, especially for small publications like ours. Our audience wants to hear this from *you*, Chloe. You're going to that game."

Chloe opened her mouth to outright beg him, but it was too late. He'd already hung up. Staring at her phone, it took her a moment to realize that Joyce was standing beside her.

"I saw your face from across the room," Joyce said. "Bad news?"

"Yeah, I'm sorry," Chloe said. "I can't stay."

"Do me a favor? Call him back and let me talk to him."

Chloe hesitated. "Okay, but he's um, a bit

brusque." She called Frank back and handed Joyce her phone.

Chloe heard Frank yell. "Frank, hello. No, this isn't—" she held up a finger to Chloe, walking several feet away to speak with him in private. After a few moments of back and forth, she returned, smiling as she handed the phone back. "He'd like a word with you."

Chloe took the phone. "Hi, Frank."

"You can stay the weekend," he growled. "Don't worry about the football story."

He hung up before she could thank him. She stared at Joyce. "What did you say to him?"

"Nothing much. I just gave him the details of our advertising offer. Frank is a smart man." The two shared a laugh. "But he's a suspicious sort. I need to get him the contract right away. Once he has proof of the offer and everyone has signed, he'll let you stay."

"That's, wow, thank you. I don't understand all of what's happening," Chloe said, laughing again. "I've never seen anyone shut him up like that before."

Joyce shrugged. "That's Sarah for you. When she sets her sights on a goal, it happens. Of course, money always helps."

"I don't know, that seemed more like a task than a goal."

"Touché," Joyce replied, smiling. "Frank is indeed just a task. But you, Chloe, are Sarah's goal."

Chloe's smile faltered. "How's that?"

"She wants you to see what everyone else sees when they look at you."

Chloe couldn't think of anything to say. She watched as Joyce gave her a small nod before returning to the crowd.

A short time later, Chloe resumed her seat next to the ever excited Kendra.

"Did you talk to Sarah?"

"For a few minutes, yes," Chloe said. "It looks like I'll be attending the entire weekend."

"Yay!" Kendra made tiny little claps with her hands. "That means we can be study buddies tomorrow."

"Study buddies?" Chloe echoed.

"Welcome back, everyone," Sarah said as she walked onto the stage and moved toward the middle of the spotlights. "Did you have a nice lunch?" A round of applause rippled through the audience. "Good. What we're going to cover this afternoon is what I call the paradigm, and the knowing-doing gap. I'd like to refer you in your binder to talk two, where you'll find a wonderful quote from John Ruskin, a prominent writer, philosopher, and polymath from the Victorian era. He said, 'Education does not mean teaching people what they do not know. It means teaching them to behave as they do not behave.'

"I love that quote. What does it mean to us? Our entire childhoods, and well into our adult years, we are told what we are to be about. We are told how to play with others, not to throw our toys, what to say to adults, to sit up straight in school, to fill in the blanks on our homework. It never stops. Most importantly, we're told to get good grades. It's drilled into our heads.

"As parents, we drill that mantra into our children's heads. Grades, grades, grades. While all schools require us to memorize facts and repeat them, telling us what to think in the process, only some schools go so far as to teach us *how* to think, that critical evolution towards what to do with what we know. A few make an attempt, not nearly enough of them, and not nearly to the degree required to govern ourselves to the best of our ability.

"We are taught what to think, but not to *do* anything with what we think. The ability to think properly and make right decisions is one thing, but taking the right action based on those decisions is quite another. This ability is overlooked in business, relationships, in homes and self-governance. You'll find that the best leaders and the best people often seem to know what action to take to get the results they desire, regardless of all the facts and figures they've been taught. That's because they're operating within the right paradigm.

"Paradigm. There's that word again. Paradigm. Let's get that sound into our collective voice this afternoon. Say it with me. Paradigm."

The crowd repeated the word aloud with Sarah. "Paradigm."

"What does it mean? To put it simply, our paradigm is our personal set of beliefs, thought processes, habits, and behaviors that govern most of our lives. Your paradigm governs the results your decisions produce. While many of our paradigms are quite similar, they are individually unique to each person.

"For many of us, our paradigm may be the single greatest secret in getting unstuck.

"Remember our discussion about belief this morning in our first conversation? Belief is governed by your paradigm. All your goals—types A, B, and C—are governed by your paradigm. The mixed results you've experienced throughout your life have been determined by your paradigm.

"You often hear people say, 'Well, so-and-so is in a predicament because they think a certain way,' or 'they believe a certain way,' or 'they act a certain way.' That's close, but it just misses the mark. It comes down to your paradigm. Your thought patterns, your habits, your beliefs, your behavior—all collected into your paradigm—will always bring you to the same place. Believe me. It's true.

"Think of your paradigm as a governor on a car. Have you heard of these? Certain vehicles employ them for safety reasons. A governor is a device that limits how fast a car can go. Doesn't matter if it's a thousand-horsepower Ferrari Stradale or a VW bus. Yes, I'm old enough to remember a VW bus." The crowd tittered. " If it's got a governor on it, it's not going over forty miles an hour. It limits what the car is capable of.

"In humans, paradigms govern the evolution of potential, the display of passion. No matter what you think, feel, or do, it always leads to the same results because your paradigm remains the same. You must change your paradigm. Do that, and you'll realize what I already know to be true. Each and every one of you is a uniquely designed Ferrari."

The crowd applauded and Sarah smiled.

"How does our paradigm have such control over us? To understand that, let's take a look at the two main parts of the mind, the conscious and subconscious. The conscious part of our mind is connected through our senses to the outside world. We tend to make decisions based only on the input received, limiting our choices by the conditions and circumstances of our life. However, we are gifted with a toolkit of intellectual faculties that enable us to expand our world. We can use these faculties in our conscience mind to accept, reject and originate ideas. This is the part of the mind we have been conditioned not to develop. It's the part of our humanity we have to take back.

"The subconscious mind is different, not the same at all. It accepts whatever is impressed upon it. It defines how we show up each day. Our subconscious mind is in charge of our actions. Our paradigm lives in our subconscious. Our paradigm is made up of our habits—things we have done before, thoughts, beliefs, et cetera. Since our paradigm thrives in our subconscious, our life becomes reduced to a succession of habits, carried out without any conscious thought.

"Where does that lead? The same results, over and over and over again. What does that look like in our daily lives? Stuck. Going through the same motions, looking for something to change and watching, frustrated, as the years tick by, running in motion. Sound familiar?"

A sea of nodding heads indicated the audience's agreement as Sarah continued. "The question becomes, how do you evolve your paradigm? It doesn't come through changing any one aspect of your paradigm, be it your behavior or results. You've tried all that, countless times. The lasting change you're looking for lies with HOW you think. Your mind loves the paradigm you are living in right now. Your paradigm is your routine. You're going to learn more about that in tomorrow's conversation.

"Today is about understanding the knowing-doing gap and your own unique paradigm. What we know and what we do are two distinctly human parts of who we are, just as the conscious and subconscious are two distinct parts of our mind. It's one thing to know what Unstuck has to teach you. It's another entirely to put that knowledge into practice. Allow that to sink in while you explore your worksheets.

"Whether you're here for yourselves, your family, or your company, these questions are going to introduce you to this new thinking and enable you to understand how it affects you. When you're answering them, be honest with yourselves. Be detailed, and write in the present tense. Make your words a reality to you. Be serious with your non-productive actions and your productive actions. Those NPAs and PAs are really important.

"For the remainder of today's session, Joyce, our team and I are going to walk around and answer your questions. Feel free to group up but don't feel obligated. If this is a solo journey for you, everyone here will respect that. If we don't get to you today, know that we'll have at least a little one-on-one time before the conference is over. We have a lot more ground to cover, and plenty of time to connect. Save your questions, and I'll be happy to answer any that aren't addressed through our time together.

"Your bigger goal comes after the conference. Spend four or five days with each lesson. You don't have to have all the answers this weekend. You are experiencing a life-changing and an intensive introduction and exploration on how to live your life, preparing you for an exciting thirty days ahead. Remember. Review, rethink, rewrite. Thanks so much, everyone!"

The crowd stood with a thunderous round of applause. The audience was talking at once, grouping up and forming little circles with their chairs. Chloe spent the next two hours in a circle with Kendra and several others, laughing and sharing their thoughts on the program so far. They wrestled with the questions in the binder, chewing pens and scribbling notes. Chloe noticed she wasn't the only one who felt uncomfortable. The questions demanded transparency and vulnerability. Holding a mirror to oneself was never easy.

Thankfully, she had a reason for holding back on the lesson. She was on assignment. She needed arm's length from the experience, and good notes on the story she was writing. Looking around her group, she was glad to see they'd accepted her reasoning. She sighed quietly. She knew it was nothing more than an excuse.

"So," Sarah said, pouring Chloe some tea at the sitting area in the small conference room. "Joyce sent Frank the offer, and he's accepted. It looks like you're good to spend the weekend with us."

"Thanks so much. Quite unexpected. Most appreciated," Chloe said. "This is an amazing opportunity. I'm looking forward to the rest of the seminar."

"It's my pleasure. Frank stressed, and I fully agree, that your story is to be an honest one. Don't feel any pressure to write a specific narrative that makes us look good. Frank has last word on the final draft, not us. If we like the story, we've reserved the right to use it for marketing purposes. Same with the interview we will be having, which will be sometime in the next few weeks."

"That sounds reasonable. I'm glad I have the autonomy to write what I want. Thanks for that."

Sarah smiled. "It's clear you write best when you write what you feel. That's all we want. Speaking of writing, I noticed during the group work that you didn't put many answers down. Understandable, given that you need to focus on the story, but I wanted to see if there was any other reason for it. You seemed a bit uncomfortable."

Chloe twirled the tea bag around her cup. "Yeah, I don't know. Self-scrutiny is weird. It's like I'm on autopilot when it comes to pointing out what's wrong with myself. I have no problem voicing my opinion there. But when it comes to exploring what's underneath, I clam up."

"That's more common than you think. A lot of people find it difficult to see past their own self-image in order to get to the heart of their paradigm. It's hard to hear anything when the limiting thoughts are so loud."

"That's it exactly. There's this voice inside that keeps reinforcing my stuckness. There's a part of me that doesn't want to discover my best self. It's strange how comforting and powerful that limiting voice can be."

Sarah nodded. "Your paradigm loves routine, the familiar. It's our habitual nature. It is the part of the mind that keeps you where you are. It IS scary to explore yourself. If I had to guess, I would say it's your type C goal, the big one, the fantasy, that keeps you up at night."

Chloe stared into her tea. "I think you're right."

"Well, I'm not going to ask you what it is again. You'll tell me when you can speak it out loud. Instead, consider this. Forget the binder materials on this first day. Same with the questions in the worksheets. Take the goal card from our first conversation. As you're going about your evening, think about everything you've learned so far, and work toward writing your goal down on the card. Don't worry about how your negative thoughts will react. I know it'll feel that by writing it down, you're making it real, which means it's something you can fail at. NOBODY LIKES TO FAIL.

"This is a different moment. You have to reach for it, Chloe. It feels safe to keep your fantasy where it is, in your head and out of sight. Out of reach enough that you never have to risk failure. Writing it on the card is the first step to believing it can be a reality. You'll see that the reality is just as safe as the fantasy.

Sarah smiled and put her hand on Chloe's hand. "Imagine you have unlimited resources to achieve it. Because you do. That's why humans have imaginations. We are dreammakers. That's why turning a goal from fantasy to theory to fact is safe. Once you decide, it all becomes inevitable." She whispered this time. "It's time for your destiny to shape your present."

Chloe took a deep breath. She was moved by Sarah's certainty. "Have you ever felt that way?

Like, by acknowledging your dreams, you're setting yourself up for failure?"

Sarah smiled and looked off, remembering. "Once upon a time," she said softly. "But not anymore."

That night, as tears stained her goal card, Chloe clenched her teeth and, she penned a single sentence. She was letting her dream take flight.

I want my writing to change the world.

CHAPTER FIVE

INFINITE MIND

Walking into day two of the Unstuck conference, Chloe understood why they'd grouped up the afternoon before. Instead of rows of chairs, the conference room featured round tables seating from three to six people. The perimeter still had a refreshments table, but several long tables also lined the room, with only one or two chairs at each for those who wanted to work alone.

For the rest of them, it appeared that working together would be the norm. That suited Chloe. Kendra and her enthusiasm were starting to grow on her, and it allowed her to observe how others navigated the program, which would give her story some wonderful insights.

Kendra waved her over from the middle of the room. Three others sat at the table with her, two of them from yesterday's impromptu group, two men and a woman.

"Hey, study buddy!" Kendra laughed as Chloe took the empty seat. "You know Michelle and Jason. And this is Andre. Everybody, this is Chloe. She's a reporter, and she's writing a story on the program. Isn't that cool?"

"Hi, everybody," Chloe said.

"Are you going to interview us?" Andre asked. "I've got some awesome quotes you could use."

"Oh yeah?" Chloe said. "Whatcha got?"

Andre stared hard at the table, then his face lit up. "The only thing you have to fear is fear itself."

"Pretty good," Chloe laughed, "but I think that's already taken."

"Really?" Andre said, mocking surprise. "Well, I'll give it some more thought."

"If you guys are willing," Chloe offered, "I may ask some of you a few questions. You can remain anonymous, or we can use your name, though my editor has final say on whether names will be used."

"I'm all for that," Michelle said as the others echoed their agreement.

Chloe smiled. "Great, thanks guys. As a token of my gratitude, I'll let you in on a little secret. I'm holding a video interview with Sarah sometime in the next few weeks. You'll be able to watch it on the L.A. Local website."

"Yay!" Kendra exclaimed, performing her tiny claps as the group congratulated Chloe. Then she gasped, remembering something. "Chloe, I was checking out your website and came across your article on that high school girl football quarterback. Oh my gosh, what a story! I was in tears by the end. What an amazing girl, I'm so happy for her. You're such a great writer. I can't wait to read your story on the program."

Chloe felt her face heat up. "Oh, thank you, that's very kind. I'm glad you liked it."

"I've heard of L.A. Local," Michelle said. "I'll have to check it out."

The others nodded their agreement as applause took over the room. Sarah was walking onto the stage, and the group turned to join in.

"Happy Saturday, everyone! I hope you got some rest last night, because we're diving into the journal to better understand this reality of paradigms.

"Continuing where we left off yesterday, we now understand that the root of our immobility lies in our paradigm, which is made up of a matrix of habitual thoughts, beliefs, and behaviors, our habits. But as fascinating as these insights are, they don't do us a lick of good if we can't use them to fundamentally change our paradigm.

"How do we do that? The same way we master anything. Practice. Looking at the top of lesson three, in the words of Earl Nightingale, author of 'The Strangest Secret' and a pioneer in the science of motivation, 'Whatever we plant in our subconscious mind and nourish with repetition and emotion will one day become a reality.'

"I was telling a friend yesterday that turning a goal from fantasy to theory to fact is inevitable, and there's no reason to fear the process. I told you yesterday to imagine you have unlimited resources to make your most ambitious goal come true. It is your infinite mind that is your unlimited resource. By nurturing your goal, infusing your subconscious with it, and fostering your belief in the reality you seek, you can fundamentally change your paradigm.

"Ever notice how the majority of your circumstances seem to line up with your self-limiting paradigm? You look around, and everything you see reinforces your belief that you're stuck. There's no way to move toward your dreams when everything around you is testimony that it is impossible. Your paradigm is a magnet for circumstances that align with it. By altering your paradigm, you alter what it attracts.

"Remember when I said the subconscious mind expresses whatever is impressed upon it? This is what I was talking about. The kicker word here is WHATEVER. Your subconscious mind expresses *whatever* is impressed upon it, be it real or imagined. It doesn't distinguish between the two the way our conscious mind does. That, folks, is our secret weapon.

"The mental exercise you'll be exploring today is how you wield that weapon. By visualizing in minute detail the goal you want to achieve, you begin to impress that goal upon your subconscious mind as a reality. Coupled with the writing exercises, time, and repetition, you have the incredibly effective means to change your paradigm, literally ALTER your reality, and achieve your dreams.

"I know what the pessimists are thinking. How is this any different than the many times before when I've tried to improve my life? Unlike your previous attempts, this experience is a measured, documented, purposeful approach to changing your paradigm. At best, those attempts provided you with temporary improvements, Before you knew it, you were back where you started. This approach alters the very foundation those bad habits and beliefs are based on.

"We need to pace ourselves in order to get it right. Small steps lead to leaps and bounds. For today, choose one or two habits that need changing. Whether it's a belief, a way of thinking, or a behavior, choose one or two that you feel are the most detrimental to the future you want to see.

"Remember our mantra, 'review, rethink, rewrite.' In your groups or alone, go back to the two exercises from yesterday. Rewrite the results you're getting that you don't want, and the non-productive activities that accompany those results. Then, rewrite the description of the results you DO want, and the productive activities that accompany those. Remember, write in the present tense. Be as detailed as possible. This gives your words power and makes your intentions real.

"Another reason past attempts failed is you tried to rid yourself of bad habits, but that's only a half-measure. You need to replace bad habits with good habits. Implementing good habits retrains your conscious mind, imprints them over the bad habits in your subconscious mind, and gets you closer to your new paradigm.

"Before you get started, there's one more important thing I want to share." Sarah pointed to the corner of the room next to the stage, cordoned off by mobile partitions. "In the corner there, we've set up a paper shredder. When you're ready, I want you to take the worksheet containing your highly detailed non-productive activities and shred them. Take a moment while you're over there. Consider what you've learned and the new direction you're heading in. As you shred your old habits, make this a moment. It is a powerful symbol of your commitment to change. The effects of this act will alter the direction of the rest of your life."

She tapped her temple. "I had my moment nearly fifteen years ago. I remember it like it was yesterday. And the power that came with it."

Chloe stared at the worksheet as the group murmured around her. *In as much detail as possible, describe a situation where you are not getting the results you want.* She sighed, trying to narrow it down to just one. Always tired, out of shape, not enough money, stagnant career, no shortage of possibilities here. Instead of stuffing those thoughts down deep and powering through like she normally did, she breathed deep, allowing herself to feel her stuckness. The frustrations of the past several years washed over her. She was exhausted and frustrated. Worst of all, she was sad. She was thoroughly beat down by it all, living a life that didn't seem to matter.

She gave her head a couple of shakes, trying to decide how to take her emotion and apply it to the exercise. She had to narrow it down. Small steps, she reminded herself. She needed a specific situation. One immediately came to mind, but it was something that she buried long ago.

She'd always been a writer, which made journalism a good fit. Her first love, going all the way back to her childhood, was storytelling. Through high school and much of college, she'd spent her free time writing. It was her favorite hobby, something she'd always secretly hoped to turn into a career someday.

That path proved harder than she'd ever imagined. Over time, she felt herself moving further away from her dream. Her pragmatic side told her that she was lucky to have found a career that was close to the fantasy. That was more than most people got. She should consider herself lucky. It was also her way of telling herself to shut up and get back to the grind. She wondered if this belief was a way of protecting herself, or just a way she was holding herself back. Perhaps it was both.

During college and her first few years at L.A. Local, she had continued to submit her work, sending magazines her short stories and publishers her fiction manuscripts. She'd had a few short stories published, which was nice, but every rejection letter felt like a knife to her heart. The rejection compounded, until she eventually stopped submitting. As she moved up the ladder at L.A. Local, she soon stopped writing in her free time completely.

She could have self-published. One day she planned to. One day. She'd been planning one day for years. It held all the appeal of a homework assignment. She couldn't help but envision one-star reviews of her novels on Amazon. The experience of self-publishing depressed her before she'd even taken the plunge.

Writing all this down now came easier than she thought it would, and soon she was focusing on the non-productive activities associated with her writing. That was easy enough. She wasn't doing ANYTHING about it. She'd admitted defeat long ago. The last few submissions to publishers felt like going through the motions. There was nothing worse than the death rattle of a dying dream.

She looked to the other two exercises. *Rewrite a detailed description of the results you want and rewrite detailed productive activities to replace the NPAs.*

Ugh. She didn't want to think about that, or the mental exercise where she had to envision the results she wanted. It was the same as the goal card. She didn't dare dream.

The energy at the table lit up as Sarah approached, saving Chloe from having to think about it further.

"How's everyone doing?" Sarah asked.

"Wonderful," Kendra said. "We're making progress. I need to improve my leadership skills for my business, so I'm looking forward to shredding the crap out of these bad habits I've had since forever. Andre, tell her about yours."

"My wife and I have twins, a boy and a girl. They're entering their teenage years, and things have been getting pretty heated around the house. We're looking for ways to better integrate our parenting styles and reconnect with the kids on a level they can embrace. I think if I can replace some of these bad habits, that'll go a long way toward getting our family back on track."

"That's good to hear, Andre," Sarah said. "If your wife is free tomorrow, invite her to join you."

"Oh, thanks," he said, "but we only have the one ticket."

"Don't worry about that," Sarah assured him. "Experiencing the seminar firsthand might help show her that the program can really help you as parents and as a family. She'll be my guest."

"That's wonderful, thank you!" Andre said. "I'll tell her tonight."

"How about you, Chloe?" Sarah asked.

"Oh, it's going well," she said, looking at her worksheets. "I've settled on a situation and related bad habits I want to change, but envisioning the ideal is difficult."

"That's a common reaction," Sarah observed. "It'll come in time. What may help is to go shred your NPAs. Take your time with it. Give some thought to the symbolism of the act. It'll make moving forward easier than you think."

Chloe looked around at the group. "You know what? I will."

Grabbing her worksheet as the group cheered her on, she made her way to the corner of the conference room. She peeked behind the partition, and finding it empty, she stood before the commercial paper shredder at the center of the space. Looking like an oversize office copier, she took in its sleek plastic angles and small touchscreen with blinking lights.

She read over the two paragraphs she'd written minutes before. These thoughts had been a part of her for so long they felt like they *were* her. She read the last line. *I no longer get up when I'm knocked down. I stay down. I'm tired of staying down.*

She reread the line over and over as her grip tightened, sending crinkles spiderwebbing across the page. Taking a step forward, she fed a corner into the fine metal teeth of the shredder. The machine whirred to life, and she watched as her past failures were sliced to ribbons. She smiled on her way back to the table, noticing that her disappointing inner voice was uncharacteristically silent.

CHAPTER SIX
THE GENIE

"I want a rough draft of your story by tomorrow morning," Frank said.

Chloe switched her phone to her other ear as she got up from the table, making her way to the hallway outside the conference room. A steady buzz of conversation permeated the room as hotel waitstaff flowed around the tables, delivering dishes from the lunch menu provided earlier.

"I need more time, Frank. I want to interview people at the end of the final day to get a complete snapshot of their experience. The best way for me to write the story is to go through the weekend myself, and we're only halfway through the conference."

"You wanted this assignment, you got it," Frank said. "We need it done as soon as possible so you can get back on sports. Your team is a big favorite to win today, which qualifies them for division playoffs. Your girl quarterback could carry them to a regional or even state championship. I want everyone following us for the story. The buzz around this team is growing. Other high schools are allowing girls to try out, and local politicians are starting to comment on the issue. No word yet from local colleges, but I want you to get statements from their sports departments. This story is ready to boil."

"I get that, Frank, but I'm in a middle of something that also matters. I'm just getting a feel for this story."

Frank sighed. "Chloe, you're not getting it. Sarah's institute is a corporate advertiser now. Your story is that the program is incredibly effective and everyone should sign up. That's it. It's a puff piece. I have no idea why they're advertising with a small outfit like us, but I'm not going to argue. The level of investment they're providing is going to do wonders for us. But there's an unspoken understanding that we toe the line. Write what they want to hear. That's your assignment. Make them happy and move on to more important stories, the stuff that's going to bring us readers."

Chloe felt the heat in her voice. "Sarah said you insisted that this be an honest piece. I think you're underestimating the effect this story will have on our audience. Sarah's right. Our audience wants a story like this. They want to read positive, hopeful narratives, just like the football team piece. This story has legs every bit as much as the football team."

"I'm willing to play ball with them, but I'm not gonna let them push me around. There are limits with their money. That's how this stuff works, Chloe. It's an unspoken back and forth, a cutesy little game of chess that allows both parties to say what can't be said out loud."

"Frank, the potential for this story dies if I pay it lip service. Let me do this right."

His voice turned hard. "Look, you don't get it, and that's okay because you don't need to. You need to do what you're told. So get it done. I got a week's worth of work on your desk, with more on the way. Have your nice little weekend off, but get me that draft by tonight. Be prepared to put this program behind you, come Monday."

He hung up before she could argue any further. Staring straight ahead, she resisted the urge to chuck her phone down the hallway. Grinding her teeth, she headed for the hotel entrance. She needed some air.

"How was lunch, everyone?" Sarah asked from the stage. "I had the BLT. It was so good."

The audience murmured their approval as Sarah moved to a laptop set up on a nearby table. The large projection screen on the wall behind her lit up, and an image appeared of a stickperson. The large head had a horizontal line running through the middle of it, with the word *conscious* in the top half and *subconscious* in the bottom half. A smaller circle connected to the head by a vertical line had the word *body* written in it. *The Genie* appeared in large font at the top of the slide, with a quote by Bob Proctor, the co-founder of Sarah's institute:

The Genie, is without question the most valuable idea I have gained in fifty years of intensive research into the workings of the mind.

"This afternoon, we're going to focus on our fourth principal, which provides a unique look into how your mind works. Understanding this will help you identify your soft spots and make the conscious decisions necessary to change your habits for the better."

"It all starts with our friend here, the Genie. Say hello." The crowd laughed softly. "Don't let the simplicity of this idea fool you. It brought together a lot of Bob Proctor's best thinking, leading to the breakthrough behind everything we are talking about this weekend. A colleague of Bob's, Leland Val Van De Wall, created the idea of the Genie after talking with a Doctor Thurman Fleet in San Antonio, Texas. Doctor Fleet was finding it difficult to treat the whole person, what they call holistic treatment, when there remained so much confusion regarding the mind.

"Most of us have never considered our mind. Nothing holds a candle to it. The mind is the beautiful orchestration of every cell in our body, how we think, move, dance, float. It is what makes us magic.

"The mind is impossibly complex. It is made up of our thoughts, our emotions, our intuition, our memories, our hopes for the future, and more. It is the keystone to the entire human experience.

"Our mind is spectacular." Sarah walked toward the front of the stage as she began to clap. "Spectacular." She continued to clap as one by one the audience joined her. "Spectacular." Around the room, people began to stand as they continued to clap. "You and your mind are spectacular!" The clapping turned into an applause that carried a celebratory thunder to it. "Spectacular!" The applause continued. Chloe felt the goosebumps raising on her arms as she joined the response. She had only felt like this one other time when she was a teenager in church. She had been searching for this connection her whole life. In this moment, with people she did not know, she had found it again.

The audience finally sat. "It may be impossible to ever see God in our lifetime, but our friend the Genie gives a glimpse into what our designer had in mind. A few profound tenets about how we think and move through the world may change your life like it did mine.

"The conscious mind receives information from the outside world through our senses. Most people's paradigm requires them to live by that input alone. They become subservient to the data the world provides. You would think that it's the conscious mind that controls our actions, but that isn't the case. Remember, the subconscious expresses what's imprinted on it. How? Through our body and our actions.

"Case in point. How many times have you witnessed people say one thing, yet do the opposite? They say they believe certain things, understand certain facts, desire certain outcomes, but their actions and behavior are completely out of line with what they say. That's because the conscious mind holds no sway over our actions. We've all heard the expression, actions speak louder than words. Observe a person's actions, look to their results and you will understand their paradigm.

"The same can be done with your own actions. How do they line up with your goals, with the future you really want? Not very well, do they? So ask yourself, are you *responding* to the world around you, or are you *reacting* to it?

"There's an added element here that's very important. It's more than just the conscious and subconscious mind, it's how your internal self relates to the outside world. It's the combination of thinking and doing. This is what makes Unstuck so effective. We aren't discussing about THINKING your way out of your problems. We've all tried that and we stay stuck. You can never out-think yourself out of stuck behavior. How many of you have been trying to get thinner for years? How's that working for you?

"True change comes from a combination of purposeful thought and purposeful action. Which brings us back to the dichotomy of the conscious and subconscious mind. How do we purposefully alter our subconscious, thereby changing our paradigm and fostering the internal and external behavior that affect the change we're looking for? You know the answer. By imprinting our goals on our subconscious mind.

"We incorporate what we said yesterday about belief. By imagining your ideal future through visualization and the practice of reviewing, rethinking, and rewriting, you become emotionally invested in your dreams. You begin to think from that place. The more you are emotionally invested, the more you bring your paradigm in line with your goals and the more your actions and behavior begin to reflect those changes. Life rearranges itself along the contours of your paradigm.

"Every time you review the program, you'll find a fresh understanding about the power within you that helps everything click into place. You are a celebration of intentionality, and can learn a great deal about yourself by objectively observing your own behavior.

"Now for some group work. I think you'll find this lesson's questions fascinating as well as challenging. These are the specifics of your behavior that require hard answers. Be brutally honest with yourself. The more transparent you are, the more you'll get out of it. The team and I will be making the rounds. Think carefully, embrace the discomfort of the spotlight you're putting on yourself, and talk things out with your group. Thanks, everybody!"

Applause accompanied Sarah as she moved back to her laptop.

"Sorry, guys," Chloe shared with her group, "but I'm going to have to sit this one out. My editor wants an update, so I've got to work on the story."

"No problem," Kendra said. "We're here whenever you need us."

The group said their goodbyes as Chloe gathered her things. She caught Sarah's eye from across the room, and nodded toward the door leading to the small conference room. Sarah nodded back, excusing herself from the group she was speaking with before making her way toward the door.

Once in the hallway, on their way to the back room, Chloe filled her in.

"Sorry, Frank wants a rough draft of the story, so I've got to get going on it."

"It's a bit early for that, isn't it?" Sarah asked.

"Yeah, he's flexing his muscles. It's what makes him Frank. He loves the advertising relationship with you, but I think he's worried about losing control or something. He's reminding me who's boss."

Sarah held the door as Chloe entered the back room. "I'm sure with a few words, I could convince him that you need more time."

"Thanks, but I can handle him. Whatever happens, there's no way I'm letting this story be published without my full effort. This is a rough draft, so I'm not worried about it. It doesn't need to be perfect, but I want to get a jump on it. It looks like he's loading me up with work as well, and there's a development with the football team I wrote about. They have a shot at becoming a big team this year, and with a girl quarterback and all, we need to stay on top of the story. I'm not sure how much time I'll have during the upcoming week to work on this. Best to do what I can, while I can."

"Exciting stuff," Sarah said as they took a seat at the table. "You know your business, and I certainly don't plan on getting in the middle of you two. You can work here in this room, if you prefer, in case you have any questions."

"Thanks, but I think I'll head home. I work better there, and I'll have plenty of questions tomorrow."

Sarah nodded. "Sounds good. I hope you can make time to work through Unstuck after the seminar, but again, no pressure."

"I'm fully planning on it. I've worked with Frank long enough to know what I can get away with. I am paying attention to what you have already invested in me. You see something. I want to see the same thing.

"Nothing's going to change if I don't pick myself up off the ground and make it happen. If I let Frank get his way and I continue burying myself in my work, it'll just be me in his seat ten years from now—older, fatter, and a whole lot unhappier." She shook her head. "I can't allow that. I need something more."

"I'm glad to hear it," Sarah said. "Does this mean you've settled on your type C goal?"

Chloe opened her phone case, revealing a series of slots for credit cards. She pulled her goal card from one of them and handed it to Sarah.

A smile spread across Sarah's face. "I want my writing to change the world." Eyes twinkling, she handed the card back to Chloe, and held her gaze. "One reader at a time, it already is."

CHAPTER SEVEN

Thinking Into Results

Chloe yawned as she made her way through the lobby of the Hilton. Having worked late into the night, she came up with a great first draft of the Unstuck story. She slept a few hours and reviewed it when she woke, sending it to Frank before getting ready for the final day of the conference. She felt it only fair to send it to Sarah as well, so she emailed it to Joyce, who had given Chloe her contact info the day before.

She was positive Frank would use it for the Friday Edition, nearly a week away. She had plenty of time to flesh it out and refine it, no matter how busy the upcoming week turned out to be.

Since Frank began throwing his weight around over Unstuck, Chloe was realizing she was more important to the paper than she had allowed herself to believe. She remembered her football article. Reading the final draft, Frank had reserved it for the Friday Edition, front page, instead of posting it in the sports section. The Friday Edition itself had been all Chloe's idea. She had authored three-quarters of the series' fifty installments. She had become the key contributor on Frank's team.

She knew the rough draft of the Unstuck conference didn't need to be as thorough or detailed as she'd made it. What was he going to do, put another reporter on the story? Not a chance. Frank was nervous about Sarah's power and her possible effect on the paper. Chloe didn't blame him. Let him sweat a little. However things shook out, she was done carrying him and L.A. Local.

She made it to the conference room just in time, squeezing into her seat as the audience applauded Sarah's arrival. Kendra and the others gave her smiles as she sat down.

"Good morning, everyone, and welcome to the third and final day of the Unstuck conference!" Sarah greeted. The audience clapped and cheered, and Kendra put her fingers to her lips, letting out a surprisingly piercing whistle. It revved up the audience, causing them to applaud all the harder as cheers and whistles went up in response.

"That'll wake you up in the morning!" Sarah exclaimed, laughing. "Thank you for that. I'm glad to see you're raring to go for these two final conversations. Let's get right into *Thinking Into Results*. I am going to talk with you about using your higher mental faculties to stay in charge, no matter what's going on around you. Our friend, Napoleon Hill had this to say about those faculties: 'An educated person is not necessarily, one who has an abundance of general or specialized knowledge. An educated person is one who has so developed the faculties of their mind that they may acquire anything that they want, without violating the rights of others.'

Sarah shook her head. "There is no more valuable quote to begin our time together and sets the perfect mood for this morning. As much consideration we have given to the subconscious over the last two days, it's not meant to understate the vital nature of our conscious mind and its remarkable ability to help us achieve our dreams. We're going to be looking through six windows of the conscious mind—perception, will, reason, imagination, intuition and memory.

"We've been programmed to live our lives from the outside in. We become victims of our circumstances, allowing the world around us to dictate our experience. Yet with the help of the higher mental faculties we've all been blessed with, this need not be the case. They can be leveraged to ensure that we each have an individualized experience—a life with our own agency, with our own will imposed upon it. And it is through snapshots of the conscious mind that we accomplish it. So let's take a brief look at them.

"Our perception—our point of view—is ours to command. It can be adjusted to better suit a frame of mind that benefits us, instead of one that holds us back. When you feel you can't accomplish something, your perception is shaping this limiting belief. It's the conscious equivalent of your subconscious paradigm limiting your progress. With practice and more practice and even more practice, you can learn to understand when your conscious is serving you and when it isn't, and how to shift it accordingly.

"We're all familiar with the will. It allows us to focus to the exclusion of all else. Your will is a muscle, allowing you to hold your goal on the screen of your mind. When you use your will to alter your paradigm through the mental exercises and work-sheets, it grows stronger with each practice."

Sarah held her arms out to her side and flexed her arms to show the audience her muscles. "See these babies? I have worked and developed my will into my strongest muscle. There is absolutely nothing I can't overcome. You want me in your foxhole, kids."

The audience rose up as one with deafening applause. Chloe cheered with the rest. Sarah was someone she wanted in her foxhole.

Sarah waved for them all to sit down and laughed. "Similar to our will, our memory is also a muscle. The more you exercise it, the stronger it becomes. History repeats itself, does it not? That includes our personal histories. We've seen it time and again, as we keep making the same mistakes and producing the same stuck results. A strong memory will aid your reason and your imagination as you develop ideas, creating new and exciting fantasies to transform into fact, and alter your paradigm for the better.

"Our ability to reason is the mental faculty that provides us with the capacity to produce an indi-vidual thought. Those thoughts drive a stream of innovative ideas designed to solve our problems.

Often considered the most analytical of processes, it is in fact one of our most creative. Who would have thought?

"Your imagination is the home of your fantasies. Fantasies are the birthplace of your wildest dreams. This Unstuck conference was once a fantasy. Until we turned it into a fact. The Unstuck book was a fantasy. The same with this hotel. The same with the next and greatest chapter of your life. Your destiny lives inside of your imagination.

"Then there is intuition. Albert Einstein said, "The intuitive mind is a sacred gift and the rational mind is a faithful servant. We have created a world that honors the servant and forgotten the gift."

"The intuition is a reflection of our soulness. We've all had that gut feeling, the feeling we can't explain. Whether it was about a work opportunity, a new relationship, or a sense of impending danger, we somehow know. 'How can you know that?' you are asked. 'I can't explain. I feel it.' We've all experienced the outcome of following our intuition. This higher faculty can also be developed, acting as a trusted navigator through life's many twists and turns.

"All of these aspects together are there to aid you. The outside world isn't meant to control you. You aren't meant to be its servant. Use these gifts to objectively analyze the results your actions produce and then bring them to bear in the creation of solutions designed to produce the results you really want.

"This practice is a cycle. Analyze your unwanted results. Formulate innovative thoughts that provide creative ideas designed to produce different results. These thoughts spurn powerful feelings that imprint on your subconscious, leading to new and improved actions and behaviors, which ultimately bring about the results you've always wanted. Results, thoughts, feelings, actions. Results, thoughts, feelings, actions. Over and over in an infinitely creative cycle.

"Its time to stop being stuck."

The crowd rose to their feet in applause.

Sarah smiled. "If you've been following along in your journals, you'll see that today's worksheets are pretty involved. This is where it gets really good. These exercises are designed to get you thinking more deeply about your higher faculties and analyze examples of their usage in your own lives. This is my favorite group session because it leads to some fascinating discussion. Dive right in, but don't worry about covering it all here this morning. You'll be spending plenty of time on this subject in week three of Unstuck at home. Flag us down if you have any questions, and have fun!"

Another round of applause went up, followed immediately by the buzz of excited discussion. Chloe spent the next few hours with her group, talking and sharing stories inside the assignments. She was sad to see it end as the seminar broke for lunch. It was a fascinating moment of the conference, and she was looking forward to spending more time on it. She wished her story had been a series for the Friday Edition, so she could continue to share it all.

As the waitstaff darted in between tables to deliver lunch, Chloe addressed her group. "Do you guys mind if I ask you a few questions? I want to hit as many tables as possible during the lunch hour, to get a few thoughts from as many people as I can."

"Of course!" Kendra said, her agreement echoed by the others.

"Awesome, thank you." Chloe flipped to a fresh page and clicked her pen. "Andre, I assume this is your wife you've brought with you today?"

"Indeed," he said, grabbing the hand of a smiling brunette, around forty. "This is Talia. Talia, this is Chloe, the reporter I was telling you about."

"Nice to meet you," Talia said.

"And you," Chloe replied. "We're glad you could join us. Andre's been a lot of fun in the group. He has yet to give me an original quote."

"Oh, I've got this," Andre said as a waiter placed a chicken sandwich in front of him. "Give me chicken or give me death."

"Patrick Henry," Chloe said, laughing. "Not bad. Nothing a little more original? How about it, Talia? What do you think so far?"

"I wonder how you guys get anything done with this joker," Talia said as the table chuckled. "Andre's given me a quick rundown of the past few days, and from what I've seen today, this Unstuck thing could really help us. There's so many applications. I think it could help us as a couple, as parents, me as a woman and my career. So it'd be worth going through it specifically for each one."

"Seriously, that's what I was thinking," Andre said as Talia stole a fry off his plate. "The whole weekend, I've been thinking, that would work for Talia and me, and other times, we should really think about how this lesson applies to the kids. There's a bunch of different ways this thinking can work for us as a family."

"Perfect, thanks for that," Chloe said, scribbling notes. "Michelle, you're owner and president of a marketing agency downtown. You mentioned you have a few dozen employees, and are considering opening a new office. Any thoughts on the corporate applications of the program?"

"Yes, the team-oriented aspect of the lessons is designed for people just like me. I read how the individual paradigms and goals can make a major impact on the paradigm of a company, so getting everyone on the same page is imperative. Our company is stuck in our old patterns of doing things. All this spells out how to get unstuck. I'm really looking forward to bringing this to the executive team and department heads. It's a no-brainer. I'll be investing in more seminars and Sarah's online resources. I'm going to make this thinking an active part of my company."

"Wonderful, thank you," Chloe continued. "That's some great insight into the business side of things. Kendra, you're in a similar situation with your arts and crafts business. I've noticed you and Michelle have really hit it off this weekend. Lots of shared interests, I imagine?"

"You got it," Kendra said, laughing. "In addition to Sarah, I think I've met a new mentor in Michelle. My biggest issue, being new to business and all, is how to market myself. I've spent the better part of a year learning all I can online about my website, social media, how to market myself and my products, to say nothing of how to set up a sole proprietorship, all the finances and stuff involved, and on and on. There's just so much to learn.

"It doesn't surprise me in the least that people have post-graduate degrees in this stuff. It takes years to learn under the best of conditions. Yet already this weekend, Michelle has pointed out half a dozen ways I can really turn my work into an enterprise, and I can't wait to sit down with her this week to come up with a plan. She's going to revolutionize my entire approach. Best of all, we get to share how Unstuck is helping us achieve the results we're aiming for. This weekend has been a blast. I'm so glad I took the Three Rs to heart and decided to participate a second time. I have learned so much from what I missed the first time."

"So exciting, Kendra, thank you!" Chloe said as Kendra burst into tiny claps. "Now, on to Jason, the quiet one. We haven't heard much from you this weekend, Jason, but we're glad you're here. Any thoughts on Unstuck you'd like to share?"

Jason had a chronic hunch to his shoulders, apologizing for his large frame. "Um, I don't know. I thought for sure I'd be one of the solo practitioners, sitting at a table by myself against the wall. I'm not really used to these kinds of events. But Kendra latched onto me on day one, and I'm glad she did." They gave each other a smile, leading Chloe to wonder if there was something going on there.

"It's been great hearing everybody's thoughts on everything. As for me, I'm just a third-shift security guard downtown. I love the quiet and solitude, but for the past few years, I've been itching for something more. I have no idea what that is. I figured nothing was gonna change if I didn't do something, so when a friend told me about Sarah and the conference, I decided to go for it. Luckily, I happened on the website just as ticket sales opened up.

"There's a heck of a lot more here than I thought. I figured it'd be some motivational thing, then I'd go back to my day-to-day life and forget about it. But it's so proactive, with actual steps on how to move your life forward." He trailed off, shaking his head with a smile. "I'm still taking it all in, I guess, but it's really empowering. Sharing the event with you all has been inspiring, so, thanks everybody."

A little round of applause went up as he blushed into his glass of water.

"That's so amazing, Jason, thank you for sharing that," Chloe said, flipping to a fresh page as she continued writing. "I'll let you all get on with lunch. Thanks again, I really appreciate it. I'll see you in a bit!"

The group wished her luck as she left the table in search of more quotes.

CHAPTER EIGHT
The Looking Glass

Chloe gathered some great perspectives from a wide variety of audience members, including some perfect pull quotes from Sarah herself. Going over them as the last session was about to begin, she felt her phone buzz in her pocket.

It was a text from Frank. *The draft is a bit light.*

She smiled, shaking her head. He was really pushing it. She knew she had delivered above and beyond on the draft. Writing was like a broken faucet, and when she was in the zone, it was difficult to turn it off. She also knew it would be far more than Frank had any right to expect, and that he still would complain.

Of course it is, she texted back. *I was only two-thirds through the seminar when I wrote it, with no quotes from Sarah or the audience.* She decided to push her luck. *Besides, it's going to be a Friday Edition front page article, so we have plenty of time.*

It took him a few minutes to respond. *We'll see about the Friday Edition. As for time, you'll realize how little of it you have when you get a look at your desk. See you bright and early tomorrow morning.*

Shaking her head, she put her phone away as Sarah took the stage.

"Okay, everyone, this last talk is a biggie. As you can see from your binders, it's called *Environment is But Your Looking Glass*, and it's on self-image, a powerful and nuanced topic. Much to my surprise, it was decided by powers greater than I a quote from yours truly should appear at the top. 'The results you are achieving are a direct reflection of the image of yourself you are holding. Improve the image, and that improvement will automatically be reflected in your results.'

"A bit wordy, if you ask me, but I do love to talk." A ripple of laughter went through the crowd. "It's quite simple. Your world is a reflection of yourself. Remember when I said, 'Life's opportunities and life's messiness are attracted to your paradigm.' Your image of yourself is a big part of that. In addition to your self-image is your outer image. Your self-image is a deeply

ingrained PERCEPTION of what you are, who
you are, and what you're worth. Since your
results are always a reflection of what's going on
internally, a diminished self-image contributes
greatly to poor results. You cannot outperform
your self-image.

"The beautiful truth is you can change it. Your
interior beauty is beyond your ability to com-
prehend. Humans require others to regard their
inner beauty so they can understand themselves
better. It's the first thing I see in a person. Most
people have little sense of the wonder they are.

"Remember what we learned about perception in the last lesson? It can be altered. And like
everything we've discussed in the Unstuck conference, you are the only one who can do anything about your perception of yourself. No one
can change your self-image but you. In addition
to your self-image is your outer image. This is the
image you project to the outside world, know-
ingly or otherwise. The way you walk and talk,
the way you dress, how you carry yourself—all of
it is the outer expression of your inner self-image.

"Some people can put on a good show, project-
ing an image that belies their true self-image, but
the practice is moot. It does nothing to change

their paradigm and help them achieve the results they want.

"Just as the perfect results you want exist and are eminently attainable, so too is the image of perfection of the self at the center of your consciousness. And as you move closer to that image, as you alter your perception, that improvement is manifested in the world around you. Focus on making that happen.

"Be warned, the exercises on this discussion are going to make you uncomfortable. But an unflinching gaze at who you are is what's required. Know that if the questions make you fidget, they're the exact questions you need to answer, honestly and with self love.

"I want to say one more thing." Sarah walked to the front of the stage, suddenly serious. "The power you have over the ones you love is limitless. The words you say, your encouragement or discouragement, your focusing on failure instead of beauty, your failure to deliberately regard them as the most beautiful of creatures, all deliver lifelong crippling wounds to the self-image of the ones you love most. These three days have not been only about you. They have been about living with others. You have the opportunity to shape the self-image of another human. Use it for the good it was intended." The crowd nodded, understanding the power she was speaking of.

"One of my favorite exercises of the weekend asks you to think of your life as a movie. You're the writer, director, producer, you're in charge of the whole thing. What kind of movie are you currently living? Further in the exercise, you're asked to describe the movie down the line, a month from now, six months from now, and so on. What do you want to see happen? What direction do you want the plot to take?

"By getting into this exercise and exploring it, you'll begin to realize that you have far more agency in your life than you believe, and this same exercise can be employed in your actual life.

"So too, for your self-image. Is your self-image limiting or empowering? Is it holding you back, or is it serving you, helping you create the future you want? This language sounds like our conversation on your paradigm, doesn't it? That's because the two are inextricably intertwined. By studying them, taking purposeful action, and allowing yourself to explore your potential instead of being hobbled by your perceived limitations, you can change them for the better.

"Dive into the worksheets and explore exactly how you view yourself the way you do, and what actions you can take to transform your self-image into something that reflects the *real* you. Give some thought to your movie title. I want to hear some good ones. Thanks, everyone!"

The audience laughed as they gave her a round of applause.

"'Fight Club, Family Edition,'" Andre said.

"What?" Chloe said.

"That's our movie title," Andre replied, to the laughter of the group.

Talia punched him in the arm. "Either that or 'All is Definitely Not Quiet on the Western Front.'"

As the group dug into the questions, Chloe stared past the page. She remembered back to Friday morning, looking at her reflection in the mirror as she threw herself together for work. Another stressful day in a stressful life, no hope for change, no excitement for the future, no real happiness. It seemed like ages ago. She definitely had a long way to go, but she found it hard to imagine being anywhere but here, in this moment. For the first time in forever, she had a path before her, one she couldn't wait to travel. There was no telling where it would take her, but one thing was for certain. She was going to be proud of the person walking it.

After a few hours of group work, the final session of the conference was drawing to a close. From the stage, Sarah called for everyone's attention, and the crowd hushed.

"I want to say a few words as we come to a close. I'd like to award Andre and Talia with the best movie title. They're here to improve their family life with their teenage twins, a boy and a girl. They settled on the title, 'A Few Good Kids,' which I think is just lovely." The crowd let out a collective "Aww," as it broke into laughter and applause. Andre stood, shaking his clasped hands over his head in victory as Talia tried to pull him back down to his seat.

"As you all know, the end of any gathering like this is really the beginning. For you, it will be the beginning of a thirty-day journey of self-discovery and improvement that is going to reshape you as a person and your future. To help you on that journey, we have some care packages for you to take home."

Hotel waitstaff poured from the entrances, each with a four-wheeled cart bearing decorative canvas gift bags. The audience exploded into cheers and applause as Sarah waved them off, calling for calm.

"You'll find a variety of items in your bag to help you along, including a sixty-day VIP access code to our website and all of its resources. The site has dozens of videos from some truly great speakers, tons of downloadable handouts, a robust forum for all your questions, and a lively chat room that will help you connect with others going through the program.

"Additionally, we've included a beautiful leather-bound edition of the binder you've been using all weekend, sturdy enough to see you through all your three Rs in the coming years, and whenever you revisit the program for a refresher or a bit of inspiration. We also added a hardcover copy of my book, *How I Magically Unstuck My Life In Thirty Crazy Days*. We have a table set up onstage here and I'll be here for the next few hours to sign copies and personally thank you for joining us. Lastly, we've included some gift certificates to a local spa and a wonderful fine dining establishment downtown. You all deserve the break. You've worked very hard. Thank you so much to each and every one of you!"

The crowd rose as one and gave Sarah a thundering thank you. Laughing, she gave a slight bow, blowing kisses and waving to various audience members. Chloe couldn't remember someone more deserving.

Later, Chloe sat with Sarah and Joyce in the small conference room.

"Just amazing, Sarah," Chloe said. "What an experience. I've never been to anything like it. I'd love to ask you some questions for the story, but honestly, I don't have any. I have a laundry list of great quotes from your talks, so I've got plenty to work with. The piece isn't being published until Friday, so I'll be working on it throughout the week. If I do come up with any follow-up questions, can I call or email Joyce with them?"

Sarah handed her a card. "No need. Here's my personal contact info. Text whenever. I'll either answer via text or we can set up a time for a quick chat."

"Wonderful, thank you," Chloe said, adding the card to her phone case.

"My pleasure," Sarah said. "Joyce showed me your first draft, and I've got to say, we're impressed. And touched."

"Oh, thanks," Chloe said blushing. "I was actually more worried what you two would think of it than what Frank has to say."

"It's amazing, we couldn't be happier," Joyce said.

"It's SO amazing," Sarah added, "that I'm tempted to steal you from Frank and have you come work for the Institute. But, I've got the feeling you have your own path to walk for a while."

Chloe cocked her head. "How did you know?"

"Number six, my dear," Sarah answered. "Intuition."

The three laughed as Chloe considered the hypothetical. "Maybe there's a middle ground. I've often had to moonlight as a freelancer to make ends meet. I'd love to write more on you and for you. Maybe there are some projects we could collaborate on. If things go the way I plan on them going, I'll have time to dedicate to it."

Sarah's eyes grew wide. "I love it. I've got a dozen ideas, and I bet Joyce has a dozen more."

"Definitely," Joyce chimed in.

"Wow, awesome!" Chloe said. "Wonderful. Oh, and we can hold the video interview for L.A. Local whenever you're free."

"I'll be in town for another few weeks," Sarah said. "Let's shoot for shortly after the article comes out."

Chloe smiled. "Perfect. I'll drop you both an email after it's published. Well, you have a ton of people out there clamoring for your autograph, and I'm back at the office in the morning. Speaking of autographs, would you mind?" She pulled her copy of Sarah's book out of her gift bag.

"Not at all," Sarah said. Joyce handed her a pen, and she glanced at Chloe with a smile. "You'll be signing these yourself someday soon."

Chloe nodded, meeting Sarah's gaze as she took back her book. "I know I will. I can see it."

CHAPTER NINE
UNSTUCK

From her chair at the office the following Thursday afternoon, Chloe waited as Frank read her final draft. *Any moment now,* she thought.

"CHLOE, GET IN HERE!" Frank bellowed.

There it is. She smiled as she got up from her chair.

As she entered his office, he began reading from a hard copy of the article, the pages clutched in a white-knuckled fist. "'As for this reporter, what did she think of the lessons Sarah's Unstuck conference had to teach? Well, this is the last Friday Edition piece I'll be writing for L.A. Local. I'm moving on to bigger and better things. And so can you.'"

He flung the pages across the room and they fluttered to the floor. "What's that supposed to mean?"

"That's my notice, Frank. I'm moving on, like it says. I'll give you two weeks, enough time to do Sarah's interview and help train a replacement."

"I see how it is," Frank said, sinking into his chair. "Your fancy new friend give you a nice, cushy job at her corporate headquarters?"

"No," Chloe said, "but it was a tempting offer."

Frank stared at her, fuming, trying to decide if she was serious.

"When you demanded that completely unnecessary rough draft last Saturday, I dusted off my resume. I updated it and sent it out to a few places. I'm now a contributing writer for the Times."

"The Times?" Frank echoed, shocked.

"Among others," Chloe teased. "The football story was a lot more popular than either of us could have guessed. I was offered positions based on that piece alone."

Frank slumped in his chair, defeated.

Chloe hesitated, remembering the good times. Frank wasn't all bad. He'd just forgotten what it was like to be hopeful, to be unstuck. "I'm sorry, Frank. But it really is time I moved on. I'm ready, now. I don't want you to think I don't appreciate everything you've done for me. You gave a kid fresh off the bus from Phoenix the chance she needed when no one else would. If I can ever repay you for that, I will. But it can't be from this office."

Sighing, Frank grabbed a half-empty bottle of bourbon from a desk drawer. "No, I'm sorry." He found two empty coffee mugs among the mess on his desk and poured a few fingers in each. "Back when you first started, it didn't take me long to see what I had in you. And you've been carrying this place ever since. I should've spent our time helping you along instead of holding you back."

Chloe accepted the mug he offered. "You helped me along plenty, in your own brutish way." They smiled at each other. "But it was only ever me holding myself back. Never you."

Standing, he raised his drink. "Well, here's to you. I always figured this day would come. I just wish I was ready for it."

"You're ready, Frank. We both are."

Clinking their mugs together, they drank.

Thirty days later, Chloe was finishing the final touches on her new apartment, mulling over the latest draft of a Times story she was working on, when her phone buzzed. Her heart leapt when she saw the notification, an email from another publisher. *Maybe this is finally the one*, she thought.

Dear Chloe,

Thank you for submitting the synopsis, outline and sample chapters of your fiction manuscript, Sunset at Whisper Creek. *At this time, we'd like to formally express our interest. If you would attach the full manuscript in your reply, our editor will be in touch to discuss possible publication.*

Congratulations and kind regards,
Multmountain Press

Letting out something between a squeal and a screech, Chloe threw her phone across the room as she danced about. She opened her texting app and navigated to the group chat with Sarah and Joyce.

They're interested in my manuscript!

YES! Sarah replied.

Congratulations! Joyce said.

Her phone rang. It was Sarah.

"Hey!" Chloe shouted. "Can you believe it?"

"Of course I can," Sarah laughed. "Congratulations."

"Thanks."

"Well, I think you're ready."

"Ready?" Chloe said. "For what?"

"The next six steps."

Chloe paused, her eyes going wide. *There are six more steps?* She thought about it a moment, nodding to herself. "You know what? Bring it on."